Business Life Basics
12 Principles

Alicia Marie Phidd

DEDICATION

This book is dedicated to every entrepreneur just realizing their dream of being a business owner. It is with them in mind that I created this book to help them build a dream. Society benefits with the creation of jobs.

CONTENTS

ACKNOWLEDGMENTS

This book could not have materialized without the village I call friends and family. My parents, my extended family and friends. They support my thoughts and endeavors. They review and edit without pay and gives me the bonus of love and encouragement.
For that I am eternally grateful!

1 BUSINESS LEADERS MOTIVATE

Motivate!

The decision to create and run a business is easy. The running of a business is where the challenges lie. Entrepreneurs are always solidly certain that their product will sell billions because it is needed by society and it is well made. This is a must have attitude to succeed in business.

However, the ultimate and most important thing in business is to have the knowledge and know-how when to seek and surround yourself with outside influences to achieve your goal. I believe each business should have an army of professionals around them to ensure the success of that business.

Business leaders should partake in personal development constantly. Read a book, review quotes from philosophers and successful people. We have included 12 monthly business life basics and we wish you much success in your business.

It takes a village of professionals to run a business successfully. Attorneys, Bankers, Accountants, Insurance Agents, Marketing Consultants/Public Relations Agents, HR Consultants, and Rainmakers/Salespersons.

I realized during my practice as a commercial litigator and in house counsel that legal liability could be reduced with these professionals being properly utilized. I developed the concept "Circle of Professionals" and share it with my clients/bosses every time. It is less expensive to hire these professionals combined than to fight a protracted law suit.

There are 12 principles a business should be mindful of and incorporate into practice. You may read one per month or in one setting.

These principles are introduced in the following chapters.

2 CONTRACTS

**Audit Your Existing Contracts And
Create Contracts Where Needed**

Often time small business owners get so busy that they fail to revisit the contracts in place to determine if they are still in the best interest of the company. When a dispute presents itself, the contract is the first evidence requested. While conduct outside of the contract depending on the circumstances may be considered, it is an easier battle if it is written in the contract.

3 TRADEMARKS

Trademark Your
Logos And Slogans

I advise my clients to immediately place the ™ symbol on their logos and slogans. It tells the world this is yours and you intend to keep it that way. The most important thing is to officially file these with the United States Patent and Trademark Office (USPTO). It is better to protect the intellectual property than to be a plaintiff fighting to protect the mark.

4 HUMAN RESOURCES

Update Human Resources Handbook And Policies

It is now the end of the first quarter. You have had time to see the momentum of the new calendar year (your fiscal year and calendar year may be different). Even if you have one employee, you should have an employee handbook and grow into it or let it grow with you.

I encourage my clients just starting to think of how they would like the culture of their organization to be when it is 300 employees and several locations. Then I share with them the legal issues to protect and or defend the culture they would like to create. Workplace culture is fluid as the laws change AND so must certain processes in a private institution.

5 COMPLIANCE

Meet Before The Need

Conduct meeting with each department monthly. Even if that "department" has only one person as the staff. Even if the department is outsourced such as virtual administrative staff or a marketing firm.

Require written reports even if it is one paragraph. This gives you the opportunity to correct "current problems" before they become a "legal issue". Always "prevent legal debacles". Practice to "prevent" and not "defend".

6 FINANCIAL

Review The Budget

It is time to review the budget you have in place and compare your financials to the same time last year. Discuss the results with your chief financial officer and or your accountant. Determine if you will need a loan to stave off any foreseeable downturn or you may need it to expand. Contact your banker and explore all the financial instruments available to your company.

I advise my clients to review the loan terms thoroughly and negotiate them fiercely. Banks are happy to lend and even quicker to foreclose because they are not in the business of tangible assets collections...they deal in money.

7 CORPORATE CITIZEN

Business Should Care
About The Community

Although a business is not a person, it has a physical presence in a community. The community is expecting it to care about their needs. Find a charity that you identify with and volunteer as a company and or donate monies in any form to the charity.

It is marketing for your company and giving back is always good. I advise the clients to have policies in place to determine, who and what they support because you cannot damage the company's brand. Think legal in every situation.

8 EMPLOYMENT

Value Your Employees

Valuing human capital is the most underused concept in the workplace today. However, here is a little secret…an employee that feels the company values them will feel a part of that establishment and work for its success.

This month, even if it is a staff of one, plan a company outing, paid for by the company. This reduces and often time may be evidentiary in employment disputes. At all times think of legal implications and therefore never purchase alcohol on company's dime and if you do, monitor the situation closely. Prevent legal debacles.

9 COLLECTIONS

Accounts Receivable
IS An Asset

The accounts receivables are assets. Treat it as such. Review internal process of collections. If you do not have one in place, create it NOW. You should have a set time that an account will leave the accounting department and be transferred to your legal department or to an outside general counsel such as me.

This work flow saves the company tons of monies because the employee's time is being used wisely. You are approaching the last quarter and the company needs all the revenue it can gather. It is better to collect some of the monies than to write it off as bad debt.

10 INSURANCE

Evaluate Insurance Needs

This is the time to review your insurance needs with your insurance agents. Hold them to a high standard and require that they explain the policy's deficits and benefits.

Determine if you still need what is being offered or if you are under insured and now need more protection. Ask your legal counsel to write an opinion on the conditions in your policy and what it means if you should put in a claim.

Start planning for the coming year. Remember it is less expensive to prevent a legal debacle than to fight as a plaintiff.

11 MARKETING

Truthful In Marketing

Simply put...Do not advertise anything false. It will cost you IN EVERY WAY from the government levying fines and consumer payouts and of course you will pay out a ton in legal fees to the litigating department.

As in house counsel, I advise clients to carefully draft the information and claim to products so that you do not run afoul of the FTC.

12 MITIGATION/MEDIATION

Mitigate Before
You Litigate

Listen to customer feedback and make the necessary reasonable changes to enhance your product or service. Use the feedback to determine foreseeable legal challenges and work with your legal counsel to reduce the cost or eliminate those legal challenges.

The customer is not always right but they should feel that they are!

13 NETWORK

Increase Your Network

Grow your network. This is not legal advice, it is just business commonsense. Attend every holiday party and gala that your company can afford. Buy a table, buy an Ad. Just be present.

After all, business life mirrors personal life and everyone likes to feel supported.

Alicia Marie Phidd

14 CONCLUSION

It Never Ends

Running a successful business creates a never ending list of duties, to do list, mountains to climb and dragons to slay. These principles are long standing and are applicable to all size businesses regardless of industry. Knowing the effect of preventing legal disasters will save your company from severe financial loss.

Take it one day and one obstacle at a time. Just remember Louis Pasteur's statement that "Chance favors the prepared mind."

ABOUT THE AUTHOR

Alicia Marie Phidd is a practicing business attorney, professional speaker and radio personality in Florida. She attended St. Thomas University School of Law and State University at Stony Brook for graduate and undergraduate studies. She has taught law classes at Broward State College, University of Phoenix and Barry University. She taught environmental studies at Nova Southeastern University and University of Phoenix.

Ms. Phidd may be reached through her website at www.aliciaphidd.com